LANCASHIRE COAST
PLEASURE STEAMERS

Pleasure steamers were once a common sight along the Lancashire coast, but are now almost forgotten. They operated from most resorts, but Blackpool with its myriad of pleasure palaces proved to be the magnet for trippers wanting a day of fun. It could also offer breathtaking scenic cruises to the Isle of Man, North Wales and the Lake District.

LANCASHIRE COAST
PLEASURE STEAMERS

Andrew Gladwell

TEMPUS

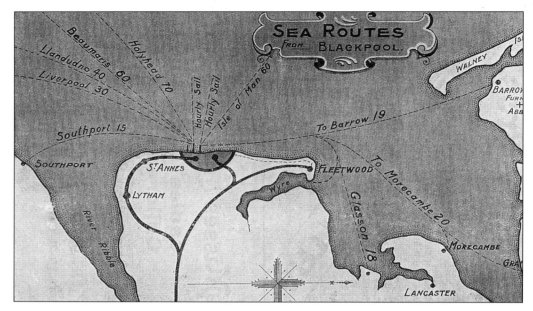

Map showing paddle-steamer services from Blackpool in 1911. The resorts of the Lancashire coast were perfectly situated to offer magnificent pleasure steamer cruises to North Wales, the Lake District and the Isle of Man, all of which were a similar distance away from the embarkation point.

This book is dedicated to the late Rose Gladwell.

First published 2003

Tempus Publishing Limited
The Mill, Brimscombe Port,
Stroud, Gloucestershire, GL5 2QG

© Andrew Gladwell, 2003

British Library Cataloguing in Publication Data.
A catalogue record for this book is available from the British Library.

ISBN 0 7524 2804 7

Typesetting and origination by Tempus Publishing Limited
Printed in Great Britain by Midway Colour Print, Wiltshire

Contents

Acknowledgements

When I started researching this book over two years ago, I was unsure of the amount of material available or indeed the interest in the long-forgotten steamers in this book. It has been a true delight to uncover so much incredible material and to meet so many people with a great enthusiasm for the Lancashire pleasure steamers and for this book. Many people have given generously of their time and material in making this book possible. I would therefore like to thank: Blackpool Central Library for allowing me to reproduce the items from the steamer guides plus other ephemera; George Boswell; Walter Bowie; Richard Clammer; Hamish Bowie; David Docherty; Mike Tedstone; Crawford Alexander; Leisure Parcs Ltd; Tim Cooper; Peter Walters; Blackpool Evening Gazette; Southport Local Studies Library; St Anne's Library; Phil Cousins; Ken Norman; Fleetwood Museum; Blackpool Civic Trust; Waverley Excursions Ltd; Frank Kilroy; George Gardner; Glasgow University Business Archives; Dock Museum, Barrow; Wirral Metropolitan Archives (Cammell Laird Archives); Morecambe Local Studies Library; Fleetwood Library; Lytham Lifeboat Museum; Joe McKendrick; L. Thomas; the Paddle Steamer Preservation Society. This book would not have been possible without the valued assistance of Tony Sharkey of Blackpool Central Library whose expertise and generous help was truly appreciated. Special mention must also be made of Ted Lightbown, the Archivist for Leisure Parcs Ltd who are the present custodians of the three Blackpool piers as well as holding records for the old Tower Company. Cyril Critchlow has been a great source of encouragement especially with his memories of working for the steamers as an errand boy. Geoff Holme has tirelessly given a huge amount of time to impart some of his vast knowledge of the Furness Railway and its steamers. And lastly, I would like to thank Peter Box for checking my manuscript and for offering words of encouragement and for his enthusiasm throughout the project.

The small pleasure steamer *Sunbeam* at Grange-over-Sands. *Sunbeam* was typical of the many small steamers that plied the waters of Morecambe Bay on short cruises.

Introduction

Perhaps the most delightful outcome to come from the Victorian era was the seaside holiday. From the sedate seaside watering place to the hustle and bustle of the larger resorts, each was overfilled with an array of delights such as piers, pleasure palaces, grand hotels and impressive promenades. Perhaps one area towers above all as the epitome of the Victorian seaside – the resorts of the Lancashire coast. From the leafy and genteel pleasures of Lytham St Anne's and Southport to the fishing port of Fleetwood, or the bustle of breezy Blackpool and Morecambe, every conceivable entertainment device was available. But one aspect of these resorts development has been long neglected – that of the pleasure steamers that conveyed happy passengers to and from the Lancashire coast resorts from the 1840s until the mid-twentieth century.

The seaside resorts of the 1840s bore little resemblance to the resorts that were to emerge half a century later. Many were just a collection of whitewashed stone cottages whilst others, such as Fleetwood, were starting to emerge and cater for a discerning class of visitor. Sir Peter Hesketh Fleetwood realised that such visitors, even in the 1840s, would enjoy a pleasure cruise and he quickly introduced paddle steamers such as Cupid, Express and Ayrshire Lassie to take passengers to Bardsea, Glasson Dock and Piel Island. However, services for the next twenty years were very much limited by the lack of suitable mooring places. The Victorian boom in pier building was the catalyst that promoted an explosion of steamer services along the Lancashire coast. Growth in the recreational opportunities offered by the developing resorts, when seen in the light of expanding train services and the Bank Holidays Act of 1871, gave the working classes of the Lancashire mill towns the opportunity of 'day trips' to the seaside for the first time and the 'Wakes Week' became a part of the life of each seaside town. Ship owners and other entrepreneurs were quick to react to the potential of this market. Soon, converted tugs and other 'make do' vessels took up the role of pleasure steamers out of Blackpool, Morecambe, Southport, St Anne's, Lytham and Barrow. It wasn't until the opening of the famous Blackpool North Pier designed by eminent Victorian pier engineer, Eugenius Birch, in 1863 that services really started to flourish. The North Pier soon found itself so popular that a new pier (now named Central Pier) was built just a few years later to cater for the 'excursionist classes'. Steamer services were soon a common sight on each pier and companies embarked upon the vigorous marketing of their services. Steamers such as Dhu Heartach, Wellington, Clifton and Bickerstaffe were placed on the station and duly started regular steamer sailings to Douglas, Llandudno, Morecambe and Southport. However, again it was not until the 1890s, and in particular the wonderful Greyhound of 1895, that Lancashire coast steamers began a new era of style and service.

The last few years of the nineteenth and first few years of the twentieth century saw troubled years for the steamers. From 1895 onwards, competition was becoming intense and soon the co-operation of earlier years, when services were operated to different places and at different times, broke down and the sorry sight of large steamers offering services to the same destinations became the norm. Steamer trade was also heavily dependent on the Lancashire cotton industry. Economic slumps, such as that in the early years of the twentieth century, had a significant effect on steamer trade.

Mother Nature also played her part. The shifting sands along the Lancashire coast meant that jetties soon became useless, with access for steamers limited to just a few hours a day. And of course countless newspaper reports also complained about the atrocious weather that necessitated so many sailings to be cancelled. The result was that most pier companies had to embark on large projects to extend their jetties to allow access at all states of the tide. This was expensive and, with the introduction of new steamers such as the *Deerhound*, the burden became too much and amalgamations became a common (and confusing) feature of the Lancashire coast steamer business. The once-great North Pier Steamship Co. was one such casualty, being absorbed by the rival Blackpool Passenger Steamboat Co. in 1905.

The period from 1900 to 1914 saw one particularly popular paddle-steamer service – the service provided by the Furness Railway from Fleetwood to Barrow. The enterprising Alfred Aslett introduced the ultimate day excursion that transported the holiday masses from Blackpool by train to Fleetwood and then across Morecambe Bay by large steamers such as *Lady Moyra* or *Lady Evelyn* for onward journeys by train, carriage and Lake steamer to enjoy breathtaking and unrivalled scenic delights for just a few shillings. But even this delightful service was short lived, being cruelly terminated by the First World War.

The First World War affected the Lancashire steamers as it did most other aspects of life. The steamers never regained their pre-war eminence. By this time, the motor charabanc was becoming an alternative. Indeed, resorts such as Blackpool offered such opulence and variety in its 'Palaces of Pleasure' that the sometimes 'lively' conditions of the Irish Sea were a poor alternative. Accessibility also led to the abandonment of services to and from Lytham and St Anne's. Large steamers such as *Queen of the North* had also been lost during the conflict. One by one, services were pruned and steamers disappeared. *Greyhound* was withdrawn after the 1922 season, *Bickerstaffe* in 1928. Clearly the services were in steep decline. Attempts were made to revive services in the mid-1930s with vessels such as the *Minden* operating from Blackpool in 1933, *Jubilee Queen* in 1935, *Queen of the Bay* in 1936, and *Atalanta* in 1937. None of these vessels were a great success and with the Second World War in 1939, services ceased altogether. In 1947 the small *Pendennis* was placed on service from Blackpool, but was soon withdrawn. The trips that were once an essential part of a holiday were now at an end.

In 1977, *Waverley* made her first trip away from the Clyde to celebrate the centenary of Llandudno Pier. As part of this she undertook hugely successful sailings from Fleetwood, Liverpool and Llandudno and the popularity of these sealed her future by showing that her potential lay in spending large parts of each year away from the Clyde to maximise revenue. From 1986 onwards, the pleasure steamer *Balmoral* has sailed as consort to *Waverley*. In the early 1990s, Balmoral offered the rare opportunity to relive the 'Golden Era' of Lancashire pleasure steamers when the first calls were made at Blackpool's famous North Pier for over half a century, as well as to Morecambe's Stone Jetty. Many people will remember with great affection the cruises of that period. However, winter gales in 1997 damaged the North Pier and cruises were discontinued. Many piers may have been lost, but on *Waverley* and *Balmoral* we are still able to enjoy the same spectacular experiences beloved by our forefathers as we cruise to the Isle of Man or North Wales. They alone carry on the great tradition of Lancashire coast pleasure steamers.

One
The Early Years

A rare photograph taken in 1867 showing a paddle steamer alongside the rather basic jetty at Blackpool North Pier, just a short time after pleasure steamer cruises started from Blackpool. The pier was later enlarged and the magnificent Indian Pavilion was built on the site where the paddle steamer is situated. (Photo courtesy of Leisure Parcs Ltd)

Originally planned as a grand seaside resort, Fleetwood offered pleasure cruises as early as 1840; Sir Peter Hesketh Fleetwood saw paddle steamers as an important aspect of his town's growth. Trips were offered by such vessels as *Cupid* and *Express* in 1840. From 1843, *Nile* offered cruises to Glasson Dock, Piel Island and Bardsea. By 1846, *Ayrshire Lassie* had also entered service.

The *Wellington* arriving at Southport Pier. Paddle-steamer services from Southport were never as successful as those from Blackpool. The huge investment in Blackpool during the Victorian period meant that facilities there were excellent. Paddle steamers like the *Wellington* were always placed to Blackpool's advantage.

The North Pier, Blackp[ool]

Blackpool's North Pier was the resort's first pier and was opened on Thursday 21 May 1863. It was a somewhat basic structure and was designed by eminent Victorian engineer, Eugenius Birch. The opening was certainly a grand affair and the opening procession included a large collection of townsfolk and civic dignitaries. The pier was an immediate success and catered for the 'select' promenader. It admitted 275,000 people during the first season. Just two years later, this had risen to 465,000 and by 1866 the income was £2,800 with expenditure of just £800.

Within three months of the opening of the North Pier, its success was clear and plans were quickly drawn up to build a new pier for the 'excursionist' classes to the south of the 'select' North Pier. Work started in July 1867 and the South Pier (later renamed Central Pier) opened on 30 May 1868. Business was poor until Bob Bickerstaffe took over in 1870. One day, he counted just thirteen people on the pier whilst the North Pier was full, so he organised a cheap paddle steamer excursion to Southport (halving the fare to 1s). Two hundred and fifty people reacted to the handbills that he distributed around the resort. Whilst they were on the cruise, he found a German band and, as the trippers returned, the band played and the trippers danced happily away. Bickerstaffe had found the recipe for the success of the 'People's Pier': the cocktail of pleasure steamers and open-air dancing sealed the success of the Central Pier for the next sixty years.

Clifton was built on the River Ribble in 1871 for Blackpool service. This photograph shows her large uncovered promenade deck that must have been a delight on a day such as when this photograph was taken. Hats and 'Sunday best' are much in evidence. But, on a more 'atmospheric day', such exposure to the elements must have been a very unpleasant experience. *Clifton* was part of the Blackpool fleet until the amalgamation of the two Blackpool steamboat fleets in July 1905. She was reportedly sold at this time to Messrs White's of Widnes for £300. (Photo courtesy of Leisure Parcs Ltd)

Opposite, above: Paddle steamer arriving at North Pier in 1890.

Opposite, below: Blackpool Central Pier. Records are scarce that record the very first paddle steamers that used Central Pier. The first known steamers to operate services were the *Minnow*, *Lion*, *Alexandra*, *Royal Arch* and *Dandy*. They were all Liverpool-owned boats that made their way to Blackpool during the months of July, August and September in the late 1860s and early 1870s. Although not fitted out to the later luxurious standards of Blackpool pleasure steamers, they provided the much-needed trips to Southport and Morecambe as well as the hourly sails beloved of those who preferred to have one leg on the land and the other on the sea.

Central Pier from Central Beach, Blackpool.

13

An early view of Blackpool North Pier. The pier was greatly enlarged at the end of the nineteenth century to cater for its increased popularity as both a promenading space and an embarkation point for the steamers.

Opposite, above: The *Wellington* entered service at Blackpool in 1871 and had a passenger certificate for 350 and a rather limiting speed of just 10 knots. She usually sailed to Morecambe and Southport, but would occasionally venture as far as Llandudno. She had as a contemporary the *Clifton*, owned by the North Pier Co. A little later, the North Pier Co. acquired the *Queen of the Bay*. Soon other small, robust vessels 'kissed the cold nose of the wrought iron jetty'. Amongst these were the *Columbus* from Liverpool and the *Express* from the vicinity of Heysham. They temporarily filled an aching void in the day-tripper market that was not finally filled until the arrival of the first real pleasure steamer to the Central Pier, the *Bickerstaffe* of 1879.

Opposite, below: Robert Bickerstaffe is the man most closely linked with the Central Pier paddle steamers. The Bickerstaffe family had originally ordered the construction of the paddle steamer *Wellington*. The pier company then bought the *Wellington* and then had the *Nelson* built. This formed the origins of the Central Pier Co.'s fleet. Robert is seen here wearing his uniform and medals as Coxswain of the Lytham lifeboat. (Photo courtesy of the Lytham Lifeboat Museum)

S. S. BICKERSTAFFE.

The *Bickerstaffe* was constructed at Laird's shipyard at Birkenhead and ushered in a new era of pleasure-steamer operation at Blackpool as she was able to bridge the waters between Blackpool and the Isle of Man. Between 1879 and 1894 she made no less than ninety trips in each four-month season. Her safety record was exemplary and she never lost one life or encountered a serious mishap. She spent almost her entire career on the Central Pier, except for one slight deviation in the summer of 1885 when she worked from the North Pier.

Opposite, above: Talbot Square, Blackpool, with the entrance to the North Pier emblazoned with posters and clocks advertising steamer trips. This 1890 image shows a paddle steamer approaching the pier ready to disembark its passengers.

Opposite, below: A view of Southport Pier. Steamboat services from Southport were very much in the hands of the two powerful Blackpool steamboat companies who plied to and from the resort. Attempts were though made to operate pleasure-steamer services from Southport. In May 1890, the *Adela* entered service from Southport. Despite a brave attempt by this and other Southport steamers to break the Blackpool monopoly, services by Southport companies were never hugely successful.

P. S. BICKERSTAFFE

It was said that the *Bickerstaffe*'s popularity lay in the fact that her afternoon sailing always coincided with the shout of 'Time, Gentlemen please' by the local publicans, which was followed by a rush to the jetty! When the Blackpool Passenger Steamboat Co. was dissolved in 1922, the *Bickerstaffe* continued sailing registered in the name of her namesake, Harold D. Bickerstaffe.

A view of St Anne's and its pier in the year that the pier opened. The steamer jetty is visible with a steamer departing from it. It is interesting to note the banks upon which the men are working and the North Channel at low tide beyond.

Opposite: The *Wellington* approaches the beflagged St Anne's Pier on its opening day, 15 June 1885. The pier and jetty had been erected at a cost of £18,000 and it was on this day that the jetty accepted its first steamer passengers. Three paddle steamers and a score of little boats took part in the festivities along with the civic parties and a whole array of vendors, bootblacks and minstrels. The Rt Hon. Colonel Stanley MP declared the pier open and proceeded with the other dignitaries to walk the whole of this new edifice of pleasure to board the *Wellington* for a cruise out to sea, whilst the *Laura Janet* lifeboat under Coxswain Johnson (whose figure was the model for the promenade lifeboat monument) was launched. The most poignant note to this happy scene was the fact that the entire crew of the *Laura Janet* drowned a year later in December 1886. (Photo courtesy of Lytham Lifeboat Museum)

St Anne's Pier was one of the prettiest examples of Victorian pier design. Building started in 1879, but it was not until 1885 that it was ready to accept its first visitors. Extensions to the pier followed in 1904 with the opening of the fabulous Moorish Pavilion for concerts. In June 1910, the Floral Hall was opened and attracted famous artistes such as Gracie Fields and George Formby. Sadly, the Moorish Pavilion was gutted by fire in the 1970s, and on 23 July 1982 the Floral Hall suffered the same fate. At the seaward end of the pier only the wooden jetty now remains, isolated as a reminder of this opulent pier and the paddle steamers that once used it.

The *Bickerstaffe* set against the backdrop of Blackpool. This photograph was taken towards the end of her career. She was the only Lancashire paddle steamer that originated in the early days of the pleasure steamers and was finally withdrawn when they were in their death throes.

Two

The Heyday

The *Greyhound* was perhaps the finest of all Lancashire pleasure steamers. Her graceful design, luxurious accommodation and speed heralded the heyday of the pleasure steamer era when she entered service in 1895.

Great Britain departing from North Pier followed by *Roses*. *Great Britain* was one of many tugs employed for excursion work whilst *Roses* was owned by the Morecambe Steamboat Co. Ltd. She was built in 1876 by T.B. Seath & Co. of Rutherglen. Small and lacking amenities, she merely catered for the insatiable appetite of day trippers to have sea excursions. The only paddle steamer remaining on the pier is the *Queen of the Bay*. She entered service at Blackpool in 1874, replacing an earlier vessel of the same name.

Opposite, above: Belle was originally built for the Llandudno & Carnarvon Steamboat Co. Ltd. After initial service in North Wales, she transferred to the Southport to Blackpool run. In 1895, her previous owners Thomas & S.L. Seed formed, with other businessmen, the North Pier Steamship Co. and the *Belle* became registered with them. *Belle* together with the *Clifton* and the new *Greyhound* comprised their new fleet. *Belle* was an attractive vessel with a white hull and heavily gilded paddle box. She ran to Southport nearly every day as well as offering short sea cruises to Morecambe Bay from North Pier at 10.30 a.m. In addition, Captain Seed would often arrange a special excursion in conjunction with the Furness Railway whereby the *Belle* departed from North Pier at 8.30 a.m. to arrive at Ramsden Dock, Barrow. Such excursions became very popular, especially during tradesmen's holidays.

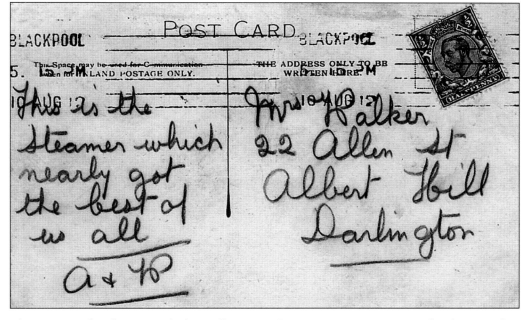

The reverse side of a postcard often tells a story. It is up to you to imagine what happened to these trippers who went for a cruise on the *Belle*!

GREYHOUND.

First Class Saloon of the *Greyhound* prior to her entry into service in 1895. This saloon was one of the most luxurious ever created for a paddle steamer. Seating was arranged in alcoves, so that semi-privacy was maintained for select parties and at the same time gave opportunities for polite social conversation. The couches and settees were upholstered in Utrecht velvet and the windows were draped with crimson silk curtains. The floors were laid with Brussels carpet and Napier matting 'runners'. To complete the effect, a splendid Broadwood grand piano was placed in the after saloon for entertainment and dancing. At the end of the saloon, you can see the staircase leading down to the First Class Dining Saloon which could seat another seventy at any given time and was furnished and draped in a similar fashion to this photograph. (Photo courtesy of Glasgow University Archives Services)

Opposite, above: The compound diagonal engines (to the left) for the *Greyhound* in the fitting shop of James & George Thomson & Co. of Clydebank. On the right are the triple-expansion engines for HMS *Terrible*. *Greyhound's* engines were remarkably powerful for their time and she could reach a speed of 17 ½ knots. One of the most important features of her equipment was that she carried an electric light plant capable of supplying eighty-five lamps, each of 16 candlepower in addition to two deck lamps of much greater strength. She was also equipped with bunkers capable of holding 100 tons of coal. (Photo courtesy of Glasgow University Archives Services)

Opposite, below: Greyhound was the reaction to the need of the Lancashire coast fleets to modernise and to cater for the growing expectations of passengers. Whereas the somewhat spartan accommodation of earlier years had been acceptable, now the North Pier clientele wanted something of similar quality to that that which was available in other UK resorts.

North Pier Fleet.

Captain CANNELL.

"THE GREYHOUND"

is a splendid boat, specially designed and built for the North Pier Steamship Company, by Messrs. James and George Thomson, Limited, Clydebank, Dumbartonshire. Her length is 230 feet, beam 27 feet, and depth 10 ft. 3 in. Her engines are exceptionally strong, giving a steam pressure of 160 lbs. to the square inch. She easily attains the excellent speed of 18 knots, or over 22 miles an hour. Along with the snug luxury of a modern river steamboat, "The Greyhound" combines the stability and seaworthiness of an ocean liner. The upper promenade deck is 217 feet long, with ample sitting accommodation, each seat also being designed to act as a life-raft in case of disaster. The main deck, almost entirely covered in, is used for saloon purposes, the first-class saloon being most artistically decorated and elegantly furnished, with seats arranged in alcoves. There are also two private state-rooms, ladies' room, smoke room, bar, refreshment room, lavatories, etc. The settees and couches in both saloons are upholstered in Utrecht velvet, and the floors laid with best Brussels carpet. Music on the voyage is supplied by a trio of capable artistes.

"**THE DEERHOUND.**"—The latest addition to the fine fleet of pleasure steamers which ply from the North Pier is the luxuriously-appointed powerful twin-screw steamboat, "The Deerhound." The "Belle" and "Clifton" also sail from the North Pier.

Captain John Cannell of the *Greyhound*. Captain Cannell was the principal captain of the *Greyhound* during her career. His brother Willie, commanded two Isle of Man Steam Packet Co. steamers, *Queen Victoria* and *Prince of Wales*.

Wine and Spirit List.

CHAMPAGNES.

	Large Bottle.			Half Bottle.
G. H. Mumm's	10/6	...	...	5/6
Moet & Chandon	9/-	...	...	4/6
Heidseick	11/-	...	...	5/6
Draught Champagne	6d. Per Glass			

WINES.

	Bottle.	Half Bottle.	Glass.
Port	... ...	6d.
Sherry	... ...	6d.
Claret (St. Julien)	2/-	... ... 1/9	6d.

SPIRITS.

	Glass.	Kr'lf Glass.
Brandy, Martell's *** or Hennessey's ***	1/-	6d.
Scotch Whisky (Specials) Johnny Walker or John Dewar	6d.	3d.
Irish Whisky (Specials) McConnell's or Dunville's ...	6d.	3d.
Gin	6d.	3d.
Gin (Hollands)	6d.	3d.
Rum (Jamaica Rum)	6d.	3d.
Liqueurs—Maraschino, Noyeau, or Cherry Brandy ...	6d.	—

ALES AND STOUT.

	Half Pint.
Bass's Beer	3d.
Worthington's	3d.
Guinness's Stout	3d.

MINERALS.

	Large.	Small.
Schweppe's Soda	6d.	4d.
Mineral Waters		3d.
Rosbach	6d.	4d.

CIGARS.

Cigars	2d., 3d., 4d., and 6d.
Cigarettes ... ... 1d. Each.	Packets 3d. and 5d.

By Order,
N. P. S. Co., Ltd.

Wine and spirit list printed for the North Pier Steamship Co. in the early years of the twentieth century. The top shows a splendid vignette of their flagship, the *Greyhound*.

Greyhound departing from Southport.

"Greyhound," leaving Blackpool.

A postcard view of *Greyhound* leaving Blackpool's North Pier. In mid-September 1900, the *Greyhound* was beached on the sands in front of the Imperial Hotel. Wild rumours soon spread in the town that some mishap had befallen her. One report even suggested that her hull had been pierced by a swordfish! After the tide had receded, crowds flocked from the Promenade to have a closer look. Their curiosity was soon satisfied as seventeen workmen arrived from Fleetwood to scrape her hull to ensure that she was 'spick and span' for a special visit to Morecambe. Civic pride was important to Victorian folk.

Opposite, below: The promenade deck of the *Greyhound*. The advent of the *Greyhound* opened up new possibilities for Manchester folk. In July 1895, a number of people in the city were eager to visit the regatta at Douglas. As a result, special trips were laid on whereby they could leave Manchester at 6.55 a.m., arrive at Blackpool 8.50 a.m., catch the 9.00 a.m. steamer to Douglas, arriving at 12.30 p.m. to enjoy approximately five hours on the island. They departed Douglas at 6.00 p.m., arriving Blackpool at 9.30 p.m. to catch the 10.30 p.m. train from Talbot Road, arriving at Manchester at 12.10 a.m. It was hoped that this mammoth excursion would become popular. Indeed on these initial trips, around 540 passengers were carried on each journey. It is not known how long these Manchester excursions continued.

Are We Down Hearted? Trippers aboard a boat named *Bickerstaffe* 'feed the fishes' as was the common expression for seasickness at the time and depicted on this comic postcard.

In 1904, *Belle* sailed to Barrow for the launch of HMS *Sentinel*. The passengers included a substantial party from the Imperial Hotel who called themselves the 'Imperialists'. Each took their own luncheon baskets and ordered many bottles of the finest champagne from the Chief Steward. As the *Sentinel* was launched, the Imperialists toasted 'Success to the *Sentinel*' and sang *God Save the King* before returning to Blackpool and Claremont Park.

Opposite: Belle and Southport Pier. Southport Pier opened in 1860 and became the second longest in the UK before it was reduced in length. For the 1904 season, the *Belle* received a new colour scheme. The waterline was repainted Venetian red, and the hull black with a yellow ribbon. The decks were painted in two contrasting shades of oak with polished teak woodwork. The funnels were cream with black topping.

Queen of the North was completed in 1895 by Laird's of Birkenhead as an enlargement and improvement on the smaller *Bickerstaffe*, also built by Laird's in 1879. She had several unique and curious features, not the least being that she was decidedly old fashioned even when built. Many found the *Queen of the North* to be quite ugly in appearance with a long open foredeck, short upper deck and funnel placed towards the stern, but she remained a popular steamer at Blackpool. She is seen here on 2 April 1915.

Opposite: The breaking of records across the unpredictable seas of the Irish Sea often produced their dramas. In June 1896, the *Greyhound* had slashed the passage from Douglas to Blackpool to just two hours fifty-one minutes. Of course the rival *Queen of the North* had to go one better and crowds of spectators lined the promenade a few days later to witness her arrival. As she approached the pier, smoke billowed from her funnel and two flares were sent up. Many nervous women aboard immediately started to sing the hymn *Pull for the Shore* whilst another reckoned that they had hit an octopus! Passengers were transferred to the *Greyhound*, while the *Bickerstaffe* towed the *Queen* to Fleetwood for repairs. The cause of the incident was a burst feed pipe. Despite great panic from onlookers ashore, the passengers were only angry that the record hadn't been broken. One passenger joked, 'Instead of bursting the record we burst the steam pipe.'

The main shaft of the *Queen of the North* was divided, and was connected for normal running by a sliding coupling. The paddle wheels could therefore be operated independently when required. *Queen of the North* also had two boilers placed side by side and a noticeable feature was the twin steam pipes that are clearly visible in this photograph. The vessel was considered to be 'over engined' and it was difficult to maintain a speed of 19 knots over a long distance. Presumably, her lightness towards the bow caused some 'lifting' when driven hard.

A page from the *Steamboat Guide* showing the Central Pier fleet. On the left is the *Queen of the North* with *Wellington* astern of her. On the other side of the pier is the *Bickerstaffe*. The emphasis in the advertisement is for the new *Queen of the North*. She has pushed the older and more austere *Bickerstaffe* and *Wellington* out of the limelight.

Queen of the North departing from Llandudno Pier. Such peaceful scenes often covered up unease over the tactics of the operating companies. One resident wrote to a Blackpool newspaper deeply critical of the Blackpool steamers. He criticised the rise in fares, the poor standard of the Central Pier jetty, the 'lack of manners' of men working on the piers, the problem of drinking on the Sabbath, the unsuitability of the steamers' 'music hall' entertainment as well as the rudeness of the captains.

Advert from the *Blackpool Steamboat Guide*.

Greyhound departing from Blackpool North Pier. On the same level as the dining saloon were two private staterooms, smoking room and bar, ladies room as well as ample lavatorial accommodation. To the bow was situated the second class areas where space was set aside for dancing to the extent of four sets. Below this was a Second Class Dining Saloon. The promenade deck was 217ft in length and had ample seating in teak wood. Music on each cruise was provided by a trio of musicians.

Advertisement from *Breezy Blackpool*, 1899, showing the interior of the *Greyhound* and promoting cruises on the North Pier fleet.

Central Pier Fleet.

(Captain HARRY.)

"THE QUEEN OF THE NORTH"

Is a handsome "all weathers" vessel belonging to the Blackpool Steamship Company, and sails from Central Pier. She is claimed to be the fastest cross-channel steamer of her tonnage afloat. Her length is 220 feet, she has a beam (or width) of 26 feet, and a depth of 12 feet. Her engines, which are remarkably powerful, have four cylinders, which work at a pressure of 130 lbs. to the square inch. Her speed is 20 miles per hour. She was specially designed and built for Blackpool passenger traffic, by Messrs. Laird Bros., of Birkenhead. On the "Queen of the North" there is every accommodation. Aft, there is a large open saloon, prettily decorated and upholstered in crimson and Utrecht velvet; also a charming ladies' cabin (with lavatories) upholstered in peacock velvet; and a smoke-room for the gentlemen. In the forward part of the boat is a commodious dining saloon, well fitted and decorated, with refreshment bar, etc. The long bridge-deck, reserved for first-class passengers, makes an extensive promenade, with sitting room for a large number of passengers. On this deck are placed the steering-house, captain's bridge, and engine telegraphs. "The Queen of the North" is lighted by electricity, and fully supplied with life-belts, boats, etc., in case of accident. An excellent string band provides music on every trip.

The favourite steamer "Bickerstaffe," the "Wellington," "Lune," and other finely-equipped vessels also sail from the Central Pier.

Captain J. Harry was the senior master of the Blackpool steamboat fleet. He joined the *Queen of the North* soon after her entry into service in 1895 and stayed with her until 1909. In 1914 Captain Harry was brought out of retirement to take up his old command as skipper of the 'Queen of the Blackpool Fleet'.

Lytham and its pier. In 1899, the *Pioneer* was offering a daily service to Lytham giving trippers two hours ashore at this charming resort for just 1s 6d. The option was also given to travel to St Anne's and Blackpool for a small supplement. *Pioneer* also offered a Thursday cruise to Lytham and Preston from Southport.

Queen of the North departing from Central Pier during the early years of the twentieth century. The newly completed Town Hall of 1900 can be seen to the extreme left with the twin roofs of the Palace next to the Tower. *Queen of the North*'s funnel is framed by the Giant Wheel erected in 1896 by the Winter Gardens Co. Both the Tower and the Giant Wheel must have offered spectacular views of paddle steamers arriving and departing from the resort. It is also interesting to note that the very first film to be shown in Blackpool was in the Tower Ballroom when Sir John Bickerstaffe watched the paddle steamer *Queen of the North* flicker across the silver screen.

Opposite: A 'floral' paddle steamer steams its way past a Blackpool skyline. The introduction of picture postcards in the 1890s introduced the popular fashion for sending a message back home to relatives and friends. As well as the familiar photographic images, artist's works such as these were popular.

Captain Clare was the captain of the *Bickerstaffe* from the mid-1890s. He had been skipper of several other local vessels and was initially master of a Liverpool tug. He had also sailed extensively in foreign waters. In 1909, he took command of the *Queen of the North* from Captain Harry, leaving after the 1913 season. Both masters gave loyal and long service to the Blackpool Steamboat Co.

TALBOT SQUARE - BLACKPOOL.

In May 1900, extensive work was being carried out on the North Pier to create a double jetty. Ten days out of every twenty-one were being lost due to insufficient water in the vicinity of the jetty. The engineer in charge, Mr Routledge, had built the Central Pier jetty and had carried out the widening of North Pier. The new jetty was built 160yds beyond the old one with a width of 16 ½ ft. The piles were driven to a depth of 16ft and formed a fender to the iron structure against contact with the boats. Piles were driven by men positioned on a circular platform that revolved wheel-like round an iron pillar. The pillar turned with the platform and gradually screwed its way into the sand. The timber piles were driven by a steam ram. Initially twenty-eight men were employed on the work. On 20 December 1900, severe storms lashed the Fylde coast. Some 140ft of the new ironwork on the jetty was ripped away. Divers tried to recover what they could, but when found it was little more than scrap. The work was completed in May 1901 and allowed steamers to call more frequently. Routledge commented that at the lowest spring tides, there would be seven feet of water. (Photo courtesy of Leisure Parcs Ltd)

Opposite: The problem of silting up at the North Pier was always a concern for the shareholders. By 1897, the directors had already made enquiries into the problem. The initial problem was trying to locate the sandbanks. Two or three years earlier a large sandbank had been found 200yds from the end of the jetty. Since that time, a new bank had formed much closer to the pier. The directors of the North Pier were therefore anxious that any work undertaken in lengthening the pier was sufficient to last a long time.

Deerhound was built for the North Pier Steamship Co. in 1901. From the promenade deck, a stairway led down to a saloon lounge that was luxuriously fitted out in crimson velvet. In the centre was a huge circular settee and revolving swing chairs. Leading from the lounge was a luxurious ladies room and state cabins for long cruises. Another stairway led down from the lounge to the main dining saloon and bar where around fifty First Class passengers could dine. The ceilings were in white enamel, with gold and maple panelling throughout. The furnishings were by Waring & Gillow of Lancaster. Second Class accommodation was provided on the main deck where a bar and dining saloon were provided. *Deerhound* was the only vessel on the Blackpool station that possessed an unlimited certificate thus allowing her to ply anywhere. Her total cost was £21,620.

Opposite: The 20 June 1901 saw the inaugural trip of the *Deerhound* from Blackpool North Pier to Morecambe, with around 200 passengers onboard. She arrived at Morecambe's West End Pier one hour and ten minutes later. The following day, she made a similar trip, but encountered problems at North Pier on the return journey. Telegraphs rang to go astern, but instead, she went ahead crashing into the piles and damaged her bow. Captain Ashcroft then sailed her back to her builders on the Mersey for inspection. During the incident, one of the Lancashire-born engineers was heard to say, 'Eh, mon, aw thowt we were bahn to be wreck'd.' It was also reported that on the return run, one lady passenger accidentally spilled a packet of salt on deck, and being a superstitious person was immediately possessed of a foreboding of bad luck! *Deerhound* was one of the first purpose-built excursion ships with steam reciprocating engines and was also the first twin-screw steamer built for Blackpool service.

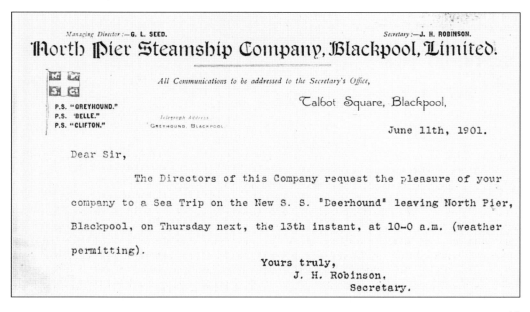

North Pier Steamship Company, Blackpool, Limited.

All Communications to be addressed to the Secretary's Office,

Talbot Square, Blackpool,

P.S. "GREYHOUND."
P.S. "BELLE."
P.S. "CLIFTON."

Telegraph Address
'GREYHOUND BLACKPOOL'

June 5th, 1901.

Dear Sir,

      The official trial trip of the New T. S. S. "Deerhound"
will take place on Friday next.

      She will leave Alfred Dock Basin, Seacombe. Birkenhead, at
12 - 0 noon, (prompt) proceeding to sea.

      Shall be pleased to see you on Board.

      Train leaves Central Station, Blackpool at 9-10 a. m.

      Your early reply will oblige

              Yours truly,

                  G. L. Seed,

                Managing Director.
                        D

The first official trip of the *Deerhound* was scheduled for 7 June 1901. The trial trip ended with a chorus of praise. Shortly after noon, *Deerhound*, left under the command of Captain Ashcroft of Fleetwood. The first vessel to cross her bows as she emerged from the dock basin was the *Queen of the North*. *Deerhound* exceeded her contract speed of 16 knots over the measured mile and was hailed as a perfect vessel. Shortly after passing Formby on the return journey, the *Queen of the North* was noticed returning to Blackpool and upon sighting the *Deerhound*, her siren was sounded and hundreds of handkerchiefs were waved in salute.

North Pier Steamship Company, Blackpool, Limited.

All Communications to be addressed to the Secretary's Office,

Talbot Square, Blackpool,

P.S. "GREYHOUND."
P.S. "BELLE."
P.S. "CLIFTON."

Telegraph Address
'GREYHOUND BLACKPOOL'

June 11th, 1901.

Dear Sir,

      The Directors of this Company request the pleasure of your
company to a Sea Trip on the New S. S. "Deerhound" leaving North Pier,
Blackpool, on Thursday next, the 13th instant, at 10-0 a.m. (weather
permitting).

              Yours truly,
                J. H. Robinson,
                  Secretary.

On leaving Blackpool service in 1904, the *Deerhound* was sold to the West Cornwall Steam Ship Co. Ltd. Her next owner was the Canadian Government where her name was changed to the *Lady Evelyn* and she was used as a mail tender. By 1932, the *Lady Evelyn* found herself on the other side of the American continent carrying out cruises as she had been built to do.

Steamer Sailings

FROM

SOUTHPORT PIER.

THE GREYHOUND.

Sunday, June 14th—
    Belle to Blackpool, 9-0, Fares 2/6 & 3/6.
        (Cruise) 2-30, Fares 1/- & 1/6.
Monday, June 15th—
    Belle to Blackpool, 9-0, Fares 2-6 & 3/6.
        (Cruise) 2-30, Fares 1/- & 1/6.
    Bickerstaffe to Blackpool, (single journey).
Tuesday, June 16
    Belle to Blackpool, 9-0, Fares 2/6 & 3/6.
        (Cruise) 2-30, Fares 1/- & 1/6.
Wednesday, June 17—
    Belle to Blackpool, 9-0, Fares 2/6 & 3/6.
        (Cruise) 2-30, Fares 1/- & 1/6.
    Bickerstaffe to Blackpool, (cruise) 2-30, 1/- & 1/6.
Thursday, June 18th—
    Belle to Blackpool, 9-0, Fares 2/6 & 3/6.
        (Cruise) 2-30, Fares 1/- & 1/6.
    Bickerstaffe to Blackpool, (single journey) 6-0.
Friday, June 19th—
    Queen of the North to Llandudno, 10-15, Fares 3/3 & 4/9

Left: Advertisement for steamer sailings from Southport Pier. The steamers *Belle*, *Bickerstaffe* and *Queen of the North* undertook cruises primarily to the ever-popular Blackpool, as well as to Llandudno.

Opposite: Postcard sent by Harry Jones, the cook of the *Greyhound*. Communication by post was the only way to contact family and friends at the time. Harry must have had just a brief meeting at Liverpool before the *Greyhound* sailed for home that day.

An atmospheric photograph of *Greyhound* taken in North Wales. By the end of June 1902, a battle was being waged off the Fylde coast. The agreement between the two rival Blackpool companies to run services in opposite directions each day was breaking down. Racing was becoming a common feature and newspaper reports noted the great alarm caused by the explosion of rockets and blowing of sirens from each jetty created by the winning paddle steamer. Some folk were woken from their beds by the noise and rushed half dressed towards the Promenade. The North Pier reacted by stating that the *Greyhound* was under orders that no racing would ever take place but racing continued and tempers raged.

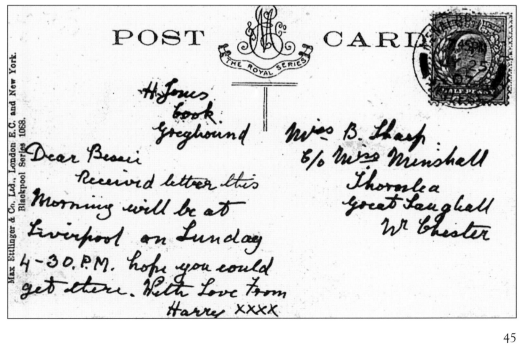

45

STEAMERS. NORTH PIER. BLACKPOOL.

T. BICKERSTAFFE.

The Blackpool Steamboats.

THE exceptionally efficient Steamboat Service is now entirely controlled by the Blackpool Passenger Steamboat Company, whose vessels regularly ply from both the North and Central Piers. Alderman T. Bickerstaffe, the manager of the Company, personally directs the service, and his long experience of maritime affairs ensures the well-being of all passengers. All the officers under his command are chosen for their steadiness, skill, and general integrity; the crews, likewise, are carefully selected. The safety of Blackpool steamboats has ever been a distinguishing feature of the service. In fair or foul weather, passengers may repose the utmost confidence in the respective officers controlling the craft that sail from Blackpool's shores.

A page from the *Blackpool Steamboat Guide*. Alderman Tom Bickerstaffe was the son of Robert Bickerstaffe and the brother of Sir John Bickerstaffe, who was responsible for the building of the Tower. 'Alderman Tom' managed the Blackpool steamers after the amalgamation of the two companies in 1905. His son Douglas took over the running of the steamers after the First World War and later became Chairman of the Tower Company.

Opposite, above: Earnings during the 1901 season for the North Pier steamers were affected by a mishap with the *Greyhound* at the height of the season whilst approaching Southport. As a result, she lost eleven days' sailings. This was combined with the late completion of the jetty extension due to the storms of December 1900 that had taken away half of the new structure. With repairs underway for most of the summer, no extra revenue was possible and the steamers had to continue their work around the tides. (Photo courtesy of Leisure Parcs Ltd)

Opposite, below: Passengers disembarking from a paddle steamer at Blackpool North Pier. It sometimes took over an hour to secure the steamers to the jetty because of weather and tidal conditions. On rare occasions, steamers had to take their passengers to Fleetwood to disembark. (Photo courtesy of Leisure Parcs Ltd)

A page from the *Blackpool Steamboat Guide*. The 1902 season saw yet another run of bad luck for the North Pier Steamship Co. Weather was yet again blamed, along with breakdown of the *Greyhound* in July after running for just thirty-two days. In addition, the *Belle* was taken off the station in the busy month of August due to major problems with the boiler. The *Clifton* fared little better. The consequence was that a loss of over £2,500 was made. Just a year or so earlier, the Blackpool Passenger Steamboat Co. had been trembling at the thought of the North Pier's splendid new extended jetty and the arrival of the Deerhound. Now, weather and mechanical failure had diluted the fears and created a raised optimism for the Central Pier fleet

Matthews, Bradford   The "Greyhound" entering Heysham Harbour. 1213/M

48

SEASON 1903.
NORTH PIER STEAMSHIP Co., BLACKPOOL, Limited.—The New and Fast Saloon Passenger Steamers. "GREYHOUND" and "DEERHOUND," will sail during the Season, from North Pier, Blackpool, to DOUGLAS (Isle of Man), and LLANDUDNO, MENAI BRIDGE, LIVERPOOL, &c. The Passenger Steamers, "BELLE," "CLIFTON," and other Steamers will make Excursions to SOUTHPORT, MORECAMBE, BARROW (for Furness Abbey and the Lake District), MORECAMBE BAY, and FLEETWOOD LIGHT, &c., and also short Trips out to sea. NOTE.—For Times of Sailing see Bills at Pier Entrance, and Local Papers.
P.S.—Sail by the North Pier Steamers if you desire speed, comfort, and every modern luxury.

SEASON 1903.
BLACKPOOL PASSENGER STEAMBOAT Co., LIMITED (Central Pier).—The new cross-channel Saloon Passenger Steamer, "QUEEN OF THE NORTH," (the fastest cross-channel Steamer of her tonnage afloat). "BICKER-STAFFE," "WELLINGTON," and other Steamers will sail from the Central Pier for DOUGLAS, LLANDUDNO, MENAI STRAITS, SOUTHPORT, BARROW for FURNESS ABBEY and the LAKE DISTRICT, LIVERPOOL, &c. For particulars see Bills at Pier Entrance.
THOS. BICKERSTAFFE, Manager.

MORECAMBE STEAMBOAT COMPANY, LTD.— Grand SEA EXCURSIONS Daily, by the Pleasure Steamers "BRITANNIA," "SUNBEAM." "MORECAMBE QUEEN," and "QUEEN OF THE BAY," (Weather and other circumstances permitting), to BARROW (for FUR-NESS ABBEY), GRANGE, HEYSHAM DOCKS, ROUND THE LIGHTSHIP, BLACKPOOL, or LANCASTER.
For further particulars and Bills apply to Mr. J. H. PROCTOR, Secretary and Manager, 4, More-cambe Street, Morecambe.

LIVERPOOL & NORTH WALES.
REGULAR DAILY SAILINGS (Sundays included) By paddle-steamer "St. Tudno," leaving Prince's Landing Stage (weather and circumstances permitting) at 10-45 a.m. for Llandudno and Menai Bridge, allowing four hours ashore at Llandudno, and due back about 7-30 p.m.
Special Increased Sailings for Whitsuntide Holidays.
Day or Week-end Fares. Llandudno. Beaumaris.
1st Saloon Return ...... 5s. 0d.   6s. 6d.
2nd Saloon Return ..... 3s. 6d.   4s. 6d.
For Particulars as to Rates for Season Tickets and all further information, apply to the Liverpool and North Wales Steamship Company Ltd., T. G. Brew, Secretary, 40, Chapel-street, Liverpool. Tel. No. 6366.

Right: Advertisement from the *Bury Monthly Visitor* in 1903. Cruises were listed for all of the main operating companies for potential trippers from the town. The two Blackpool companies were particularly boastful of their services and vessels.

Opposite, below: Greyhound entering Heysham harbour. *Greyhound* was principally placed on the Douglas and Llandudno services. After war service as a minesweeper named *Greyhound II*, she resumed her Isle of Man and Llandudno services as well as calling at such places as Heysham. In April 1923, she was purchased by Wilson & Reid for further service at Belfast Lough before being sold in March 1925 to Turkish owners.

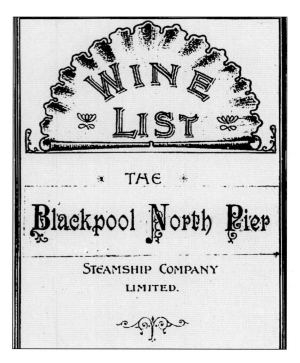

Wine list cover used by the North Pier Steamship Co.

THE BLACKPOOL NORTH PIER STEAMSHIP Coy., LTD.

WINE · LIST

CHAMPAGNES

	Bottle.	Half-Bottle.
LOUIS ROEDERER'S "CARTE BLANCHE,"	9s. 6d.	5s. 0d.
G. H. MUMM'S "FIRST QUALITY,"	9s. 0d.	5s. 0d.
MOET AND CHANDON'S,	8s. 6d.	4s. 6d.
HEIDSIECK'S "DRY MONOPOLE,"	10s. 6d.	5s. 6d.
CHATEAU DE CONDE SILLERY,	2s. 3d. per ¼ Bottle.	

BURGUNDY

BEAUNE,	4s. 0d.	2s. 6d.
SPARKLING BURGUNDY,	5s. 6d.	3s. 0d.

STILL HOCKS

NIERSTEINER,	3s. 0d.	2s. 0d.
HOCKHEIMER,	4s. 0d.	2s. 6d.

WINES

SHERRY—MEDIUM DRY,	5s. 0d.	2s. 6d.
PORT,	5s. 0d.	2s. 6d.

CLARETS

ST. JULIEN,	4s. 0d.	2s. 0d.
MEDOC,	3s. 0d.	1s. 6d.

WINES AND SPIRITS

	Glass.	Half Glass.
BRANDY—MARTELL'S & HENNESSY'S,	1s.	6d.
BRANDY,	8d.	4d.
SCOTCH WHISKY, "GLENLIVET,"	6d.	3d.
IRISH WHISKY, "J. JAMESON'S,"	6d.	3d.
RUM, "JAMAICA,"	6d.	3d.
GIN, "HOLLANDS" AND "LONDON,"	6d.	3d.
PORT, SHERRY, AND CLARET,	6d.	3d.

LIQUEURS

MARASCHINO,	6d.
CURACOA,	6d.
BENEDICTINE,	6d.
CHARTREUSE,	6d.

	Large.	Small.
BASS'S BEER AND GUINNESS'S STOUT,	6d.	4d.
SCHWEPPE'S MINERAL WATERS,	6d.	3d.
CANTRELL & COCHRANE'S GINGER ALE,	6d.	3d.
CHOICE CIGARS,		4d.

HERON & BREARLEY, LTD., *Caterers.*

Wine list for the North Pier Steamship Co. It is interesting to note that the company's name has been pasted over the top of the original printed heading of 'Liverpool and North Wales Steamship Company Limited' and the names of the pleasure steamers *St Tudno* and *St Elvies*. Presumably, catering was offered to both steamer companies by the same catering company of Heron & Brierley.

Hotel Metropole,
BLACKPOOL.

Toast ...." The King "...........CHAIRMAN.
Toast ..." The Firm "...Mr. J. E. HAMILTON.

Chairman · · J. McKECHNIE, Esq.

Carruthers, Printer.

Vickers, Sons, & Maxim,
LIMITED,
BARROW-IN-FURNESS.

Officials'
AND
Foremen's Outing,
TO
BLACKPOOL,
Saturday, July 2nd, 1904.

Programme for an outing aboard the *Greyhound* for officials and foremen employed by Vickers Sons & Maxim of Barrow to Blackpool on Saturday 2 July 1904.

Lune (left) and *Greyhound* (right) viewed from the Central Pier jetty. The Central Pier relied heavily on the steamboat traffic unlike the other two piers that were primarily entertainment piers. In the early years of the twentieth century, there was strong agitation amongst shareholders to both increase the length of the jetty and to acquire a new steamer.

By November 1903, Alderman Tom Bickerstaffe, voiced the idea that both steamer companies should amalgamate. The intense rivalry of the past two years was obviously proving to be detrimental to both companies. Although such monopolies were objectionable, it was obvious that it would now benefit all concerned. At the later meeting of the North Pier Steamer Co.'s shareholders, an entirely different and hostile viewpoint was taken. They scotched such suggestions and went as far as stating that no arrangements should be entered into in the next season over deployment of the large steamers. However, the company was failing and the liquidators were soon called in.

Blackpool.

By July 1904, the amalgamation of the two Blackpool steamboat companies seemed to be as far away as ever. Both companies were still running similar cruises at the same time, even at quiet times during the season. The co-operation of earlier years was just not happening. This was particularly evident at Southport when trips were offered to Blackpool for several days in succession. Then several were offered to Llandudno! The Southport trade couldn't sustain such an 'overcrowded' service.

Opposite: Passengers aboard a steamer at North Pier. The initials 'GW' and 'WP' often appeared on Blackpool steamer handbills. The explanation is simple: these letters stood for 'God Willing' or 'Weather Permitting'! Newspapers of the period were full of stories detailing adventures at sea. For example, on 31 May 1901, around 250 passengers boarded the *Clifton* at North Pier. After half an hour, the advertised cruise to Morecambe Bay was cancelled, and passengers 'suffered' for five hours as attempts were made to get the steamer alongside the pier. Eventually, the *Clifton* made for Fleetwood at 7.35 p.m. Passengers were said to have been 'terrified' and many collapsed in a 'dead swoon'. On arrival at Fleetwood, the sick, hungry and angry were offered a train return to Blackpool. (Photo courtesy of Leisure Parcs Ltd)

On 3 July 1905, the sale of the North Pier Steamship Co.'s fleet was announced when the Blackpool Passenger Steamboat Co. completed the purchase of the *Greyhound*, *Belle*, and *Clifton*. The price of the *Greyhound* was £7,725. The *Deerhound* was sold for further service elsewhere for around £9,000. The sale of the entire North Pier fleet had produced £18,800 for the liquidators.

A fully laden *Bickerstaffe* approaching Blackpool's Central Pier.

THE Alexandra ...
Restaurant

Victoria St., Blackpool.

And ...
Hammerton
Street,
BURNLEY.

Special
Attention
and
Terms
to
Parties.

THE most commodious and Central Restaurant in Blackpool, being one minute's walk from the Sea, Tower, Palace, Winter Gardens, the Grand Theatre, and Central Station.

Accommodation for all kinds of Catering, and for Parties of any description.

BILLIARD ROOM
EIGHT TABLES
By Burroughs & Watts.

100 up, 6d.   50 up, 3d.

T. CALVERLEY, Proprietor.

Advertisement for the Alexandra Restaurant in Blackpool (now the site of Boot's) taken from the *Steamboat Guide* of 1906. The guides contained numerous adverts for products and services in each town and included straw hats, cycles and artificial teeth.

The St Anne's lifeboat, the *Brothers*, is seen here on a practice launch during the early years of the twentieth century. She is passing the pier jetty with what is believed to be the *Wellington* passing in the background. (Photo courtesy of the Lytham Lifeboat Museum)

PADDLING AT BLACKPOOL.

Paddling hasn't changed at Blackpool since this photograph was taken just before the First World War. It is interesting to note the enormous length of the North Pier jetty compared with the initial one in the 1860s. At the end of the jetty you can see the steps to the lower level used for disembarkation at low tide. The beach is also busy with some of the familiar sailing craft that plied from the central beach for a trip 'round the bay'. Several survived into the 1970s when wagons took passengers out to the awaiting motor boats for a sail.

Opposite: The steamer jetty at St Anne's Pier. The pier was 315yds long with a 40ft jetty that was attached to the end at an angle. The steamer had three landing levels that allowed access at all states of the tide. Many onlookers can be seen staring out to sea – looking at the sailing vessels that provided short cruises. Large pleasure steamers also called, but this service ceased in the early twentieth century due to the silting up of the channel. (Reproduced by permission of Lancashire County Library, North Division, St Anne's Library)

A steamer departing from Lytham Pier. Lytham was a popular place of residence for the wealthy, with an abundance of charming and impressive villas lining its leafy streets. Lytham Pier had opened on Easter Monday 1865 and was 916ft in length. It had an eventful life and was used until the early twentieth century by the pleasure steamers from Blackpool, Preston and Southport. It closed in 1938 and, despite some attempts to halt the decline, became an eyesore and was demolished by the council in the spring of 1960. It had a somewhat 'functional' appearance and lacked the beauty of its neighbour at St Anne's. (Reproduced by permission of Lancashire County Library, North Division, St Anne's Library)

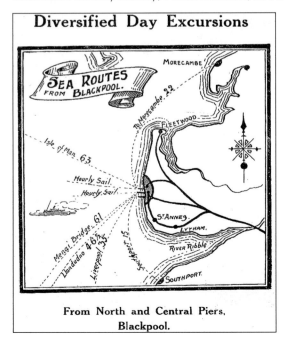

Map showing the range of day excursions from Blackpool in the days before the First World War along with the distance to each destination measured in miles.

The North Pier Steamship Co.'s *Greyhound* was the *Queen of the North*'s greatest competitor between 1895 and 1905. *Greyhound* was the larger, with a more pleasing appearance having an extensive and continuous promenade deck. Both paddle steamers performed the same type of excursions from Blackpool. After the 1905 takeover, the steamers were all painted with plain buff funnels and sailed from both piers. During the mid-season, *Queen of the North* mainly worked the Douglas service from Blackpool and/or Southport, while the *Greyhound* did most of the Menai Bridge and Llandudno excursions as well as sailing frequently to places such as Morecambe and Liverpool. It was left to the *Queen of the North* to do the Llandudno and Liverpool trips especially in late and early season.

Line drawing of the *Greyhound* drawn about 1903.

NORTH PIER STEAMSHIP CO. BLACKPOOL LIMITED.

Steamer *Greyhound*

June 5 190 4

OUTWARD.

Dear Sirs,

The Steamer *Greyhound* under my command,
sailed from .... at .... m. on the ....
and arrived at .... at .... m. on the ....
Length of passage .... hours, ... minutes, with .... passengers
Wind .... Weather ....
Course .... Draft forward .... Aft ....

Passengers consisted of :—   Total

1st Class (single) ....   2nd Class (single) ....
  „   (return) ....   „   (return) ....
  „   (passes) ....   „   (passes) ....
Total 1st Class Pass. ....   Total 2nd Class Pass. ....

Passed : ....
....
....
....

HOMEWARD.

Sailed from .... at .... m. on the ....
and arrived .... at .... m. on the ....
Length of passage .... hours, ... minutes, with .... passengers
Wind .... Weather ....
Course .... Draft forward .... Aft ....

Passed : ....

Remarks : *At Preston under repairs*
....
....
....

Your obedient Servant,

Wm Beckerstaffe Master.

THIS TO BE SENT TO THE COMPANY'S OFFICE.

A page from the log of the North Pier's
Greyhound in June 1904.

TO THE SHAREHOLDERS OF THE

North Pier Steamship Co. Ltd.

BLACKPOOL.

DEAR SIR OR MADAM,

You are earnestly invited to attend a Special Preliminary, but Informal Meeting of the Shareholders, to be held at the Station Hotel, Blackpool, at 3·0 p.m., Saturday, October 29th, 1904.

Letter distributed to the shareholders of the North Pier Steamship Co. Ltd announcing the meeting to consider the amalgamation of the two Blackpool fleets. This was finally achieved on 3 July 1905.

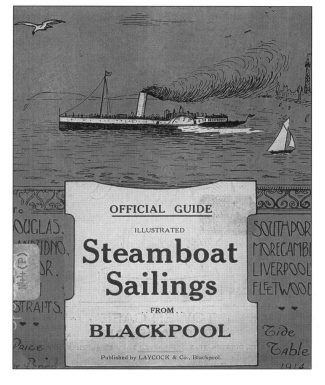

Cover page from the *Blackpool Steamboat Guide* detailing cruises for the 1914 season. These guides were purchased for a penny and included details of the all the cruises available along with comprehensive information on destinations such as Douglas and Llandudno. They also included a large number of advertisements.

At Fleetwood, a new company was formed in 1900 called The Fleetwood Steam Pleasure Boat Co. The main vessel was the small screw steamer *Pioneer*. She lasted for five years. Cruises were also offered by the tugs Fylde (pictured here) along with the *Cleveleys* and the *Lune* – a small railway company paddle steamer. One of the most notable cruises that these little ships undertook was to see the fourteen warships of the Royal Navy's Channel Fleet anchored in the Lune Deeps as part of a tour of British ports in August 1907.

"Sunbeam" at Grange Pier.

A postcard view of *Sunbeam* at Clare House Pier, Grange-over-Sands. *Sunbeam* was built by T.B. Seath & Co. of Rutherglen in 1885 for the Morecambe Steamboat Co. The company had originally built the Bayley Lane Pier for their steamers, but in 1893 Clare House Pier was constructed to take larger steamers. Clare House Pier was reportedly purchased and removed by Richard Bush from Piel and re-erected at Grange-over-Sands. The steamer service lasted until around 1910 and the *Sunbeam* was the last steamer to make the call. Many of the Grange residents were happy to see the demise of the pleasure steamer trade as they felt that they bought hordes of mostly Yorkshire holidaymakers to the quiet and fashionable resort.

Opposite: Short pleasure-steamer cruises were offered from Fleetwood ferry beach to places like Wardley's Hotel, four miles upriver, where a small pier had been built to accommodate trippers eager for refreshments.

Clare Lane Pier, Grange-over-Sands. The town was a popular calling point for the Morecambe steamers. Large 'prawner' yachts brought many people to Grange as part of a 'round the bay' trip, but the waters (or lack of) were not always so tranquil and violent storms often battered such small piers in the winter. The two piers at Grange-over-Sands were very similar in appearance to some of the small Clyde piers such as Tighnabruaich.

A postcard view of *Sunbeam*. She had a relatively short life cruising in Morecambe Bay and finished her career in 1909.

The Lune photographed at Fleetwood on a cruise from Blackpool. Lune was built in 1892 and undertook a number of pleasure trips and summer evening cruises.

Lune was sold to Cosen's of Weymouth in June 1913 and renamed *Melcombe Regis*. She is seen here at Weymouth where she served until the outbreak of the First World War. During the conflict, she served as an Admiralty tender. She was laid up in November 1923 and then, under her own steam, sailed to the breakers at Felixstowe.

The Irish Sea is notoriously moody. This photograph of Blackpool North Pier was taken from Princess Parade on 21 September 1929 and explains why pleasure steamer sailings were often affected by weather. Newspapers of the time were often full of horrific stories when the steamers were stranded at sea and unable to land passengers at the piers.

BLACKPOOL PASSENGER STEAMBOAT COMPANY, LIMITED.

SEA EXCURSIONS FROM THE

NORTH AND CENTRAL PIERS

By the Favourite Passenger Steamers, BICKERSTAFFE AND WELLINGTON.

GOOD FRIDAY

Central Pier	**North Pier**
Hourly Sails from 9-30 a.m to 1-30 p.m.	Hourly Sails from 9-30 a.m. to 2-0 p.m.
Fleetwood, 2-30 (To Return by Rail or Electric Car).	Fleetwood at 3-0 (To Return by Rail or Electric Car).

SATURDAY, APRIL 22nd

Central Pier	**North Pier**
Hourly Sails from 9-30 a.m. to 2-0 p.m.	Hourly Sails all Day.
Fleetwood, 3-0 (To Return by Rail or Electric Car).	

EASTER SUNDAY, APRIL 23rd

Central Pier	**North Pier**
Grand Sea Cruises in Morecambe Bay at 10-30, arriving back at 12-30 prompt, and at 2-30, arriving back at 4-30.	Grand Sea Cruises in Morecambe Bay at 10-30, arriving back at 12-30, and at 2-45, arriving back at 4-45.

MONDAY, APRIL 24th

Central Pier	**North Pier**
Hourly Sails from 10-0 a.m. to 1-15 p.m. Grand Sea Cruise in Morecambe Bay at 2-30, arriving back at 4-30.	Hourly Sails all Day.

TUESDAY, APRIL 25th

Central Pier	**North Pier**
Hourly Sail, 11-15.	Grand Sea Cruise in Morecambe Bay at 10-45, arriving back at 12-30.

FARES.

Hourly Sails including Pier Entrance	7d.	Saloon 10d
Sea Cruises in Morecambe Bay, including Pier Entrance	1/1	„ 1/7
Fleetwood, (to return by Rail or Electric Car) Circular Trip, Boat and Car............	1/4	„ 1/10

Passengers returning via Fleetwood must change their Tickets, if coming by rail at the Railway Station, if coming by Electric Car at the Tramway Booking Office.

Liberty is reserved, without previous notice, to withdraw any of the above trips, or alter the advertised times of Sailings should weather or unforseen circumstances so require.

For further information respecting the above Sailings, apply at entrance of the North or Central Piers.

TOM BICKERSTAFFE, Manager.

Hargreaves & Wilson, Euston Street and New Road, Blackpool.

Handbill for the Blackpool Passenger Steamboat Co.'s sailings from the North and Central Piers over Easter 1905. This was the first year of amalgamation of the two steamer fleets.

Despite looking dated, *Queen of the North* retained her immense popularity right up to the outbreak of the First World War. This is shown by the fact that she was re-boilered in the winter of 1913-1914 by Laird's at Birkenhead. During the First World War, she was stationed in the Harwich Minesweeping Division. During this time she caused quite a stir by reason of her great speed. Sadly, on 20 July 1917 she struck a mine two miles off Orford Ness and sank with the loss of seven officers and twenty-two men. *Queen of the North*, under the command of Lieutenant Cook, had been covering for the turbine minesweeper *St Seriol* whilst she was undergoing work at Hull. At the moment when *St Seriol* returned, she arrived just in time to see the famous Blackpool steamer sink under a great cloud of smoke and debris. She could only manage to pick up a few lucky survivors. Amongst those lost were the *Queen*'s master, Lieutenant Cook.

Opposite: A postcard view: *Queen of the North* sometimes offered cruises from Barrow. Tom Bickerstaffe's boastful advertising in August 1902 offered a cruise from Barrow to Blackpool with thirteen hours ashore. The ship departed after the curtain came down on evening performances in the huge array of theatres. The combination of steamer and theatre ensured that the business interests of the Bickerstaffe family were fully satisfied.

Holidaymakers at the Pier Head on North Pier Blackpool. This area was adjacent to the jetty and passengers would have passed by when arriving or departing by pleasure steamer. North Pier was always the more 'select' pier and was the scene of the so-called 'Fine Feather Parade' when fine clothes were shown off to best advantage to fellow promenaders.

Last Ship at S'port 1925

Pier Head, Southport. B. 224.

Greyhound at Southport Pier. The postcard is labelled as being the last ship at Southport in 1925. Pleasure-steamer services ceased relatively early all along the Lancashire coast as shifting sands and falling trade took hold.

Directors of the Blackpool Passenger Steamboat Co. reluctantly made the following announcement in the spring of 1915: 'Owing to the restrictions imposed by the Admiralty, and to other difficulties, the board have reluctantly decided not to run their usual summer sailings.' By this time, mines were becoming a major problem for the Admiralty and many paddle steamers were requisitioned for war service. *Greyhound* was one of the first to be commissioned (1 October 1915 until 14 May 1919) as well as others such as *Belle* and *Bickerstaffe*. *Queen of the North* was also requisitioned and was subsequently lost during the conflict.

Opposite: Pleasure steamers alongside Blackpool North Pier in the days before the First World War.

The *Greyhound* was perhaps the greatest of the Lancashire coast pleasure steamers. Her withdrawal signalled the end of the heyday of the Lancashire coast steamers.

Three
The Lakeland Connection

From 1900 until the outbreak of the First World War, one of the most popular paddle-steamer cruises was offered by the Furness Railway on their service from Fleetwood to Barrow. They also provided Lakeland tours that offered trippers an excursion to view the scenic beauties of the Lake District. This image shows the *Lady Moyra* approaching Fleetwood. Note that she has her original name of *Gwalia* on her bow.

In 1895, Alfred Aslett became the General Manager of the Furness Railway and immediately started to introduce new initiatives to boost the ailing railway. He decided to open up the tourist potential of the railway and in particular he wanted to attract the huge market offered by Blackpool. The working-class tourist from industrial Lancashire might not want to spend a week's holiday in the Lakes, but they might enjoy a day there. Aslett devised a circular day tour using the railway that began with a thrilling steamer cruise across Morecambe Bay.

The Furness Railway from the start developed an ambitious and novel advertising programme for their services. This cart was yet another way that they advertised. It was pushed through the streets of Blackpool to promote the steamer service and must have caused quite a stir.

Having completed plans for the service a new paddle steamer, the *Lady Evelyn* was ordered from J. Scott & Co. of Kinghorn. She would have been ready for service in early 1900, but unfortunately her builders were in serious financial difficulty and she was therefore delayed. She was eventually launched on 10 August and was named after the wife of Mr Victor Cavendish, a director of the Furness Railway.

Lady Evelyn sailed late in August in an unfinished condition via the north route from the Forth and stopped at Oban for coal on her way. It is assumed that fitting out was completed by a local company. It is possible that she made a trial run at the end of 1900, but her inaugural passenger cruise was on Good Friday, 5 April 1901. On Easter Monday, the weather was horrendous and *Lady Evelyn*, with around 100 passengers aboard, was struck by heavy seas as soon as she left the Walney Channel. She suffered damage and returned to Barrow.

Opposite, top: Lady Evelyn was a small paddle steamer being only 170ft long. When built, she had an open foredeck and carried a main mast. Her speed of 15 knots allowed her to make the short sixteen-mile crossing between Fleetwood and Barrow in one and a quarter hours. Two return trips were completed each day leaving Barrow at 9.00 a.m. and 1.45 p.m. and from Fleetwood at 10.45 p.m. and 6.00 p.m. Sailings in 1901 continued until the latter part of September. Revenue was good with 29,165 passengers carried and takings of £1,798.

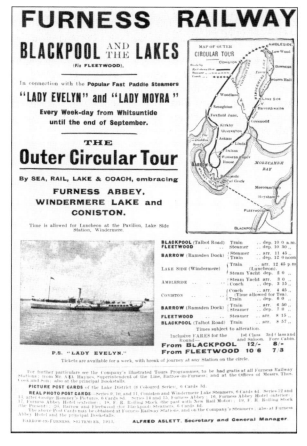

A page from a Furness Railway guide book. The Furness Railway participated in a number of major international exhibitions before the First World War. Their substantial stand contained a model of the *Lady Evelyn* (now at the Dock Museum, Barrow). In October 1908, over 8,000 visitors a day passed the stand, taking a precise 51,954 guidebooks and purchasing over 3,000 postcards.

Lady Evelyn at Barrow just before she was rebuilt. The submarine in the foreground was number *A1* and was sunk on naval manoeuvres on 18 March 1904 after being struck by the liner *Berwick Castle* off the Isle of Wight. The writer states, 'This is a picture of the ill-fated *A1* submarine. I have seen her go down under the water and up again while on trials. We know two gone down on it, won't be up for another week yet.'

As well as rebuilding the *Lady Evelyn*, the company purchased P&A Campbell's *Lady Margaret* in 1903. She was a larger steamer at 210ft long. With two steamers, it was now possible for the Furness Railway to experiment with services and during June 1903, *Lady Evelyn* was placed on a Barrow to Morecambe service. Later in July, *Lady Margaret* was used to provide a Barrow to Southport service. The 1903 season was a great success and fully justified the acquisition of the *Lady Margaret*. A total of 58, 670 passengers had used the Fleetwood to Barrow service, with 3,792 booking the circular tour ticket for the Lakes. Additionally, the new Morecambe service had resulted in 4,554 passengers carried on just twenty-nine trips and contributing another £256 of revenue.

Opposite: In view of the growing number of passengers carried in the 1902 and 1903 seasons, it was decided to lengthen the *Lady Evelyn* by 30ft as well as building up the fore-deck flush with the promenade deck. During the alterations, the main mast was removed. The work was carried out by Vickers Sons & Maxim Ltd at Barrow in 1904 at a cost of £6,550. After the work, she could carry 714 passengers on a Class III certificate.

Passengers observe the captain of the *Lady Evelyn*. In 1905, a Barrow to Heysham service was introduced three times a week. Later experimental trips were also made to Blackpool and Liverpool. *Lady Margaret* also made occasional visits to Southport from Barrow, mostly on Sundays. On 3 April 1908, it was announced that *Lady Margaret* had been sold for £14,000. Her disposal was somewhat curious as she was sold to the Admiralty for whom she provided another fifteen years of service. The local press speculated that a new steamer was to be built. Whether turbine or paddle she was going to be a 'twenty knotter'. Such a steamer may have been planned, but a severe trade depression in the area intervened and such rumours never materialised.

Lady Evelyn arriving at Fleetwood was a full complement of passengers. By looking at a map of Morecambe Bay, it is clear that the distance by sea from Fleetwood to Barrow was considerably shorter than the seventy miles or more using several indirect railway lines. Furthermore, at the time road transport was largely restricted to horse drawn vehicles. Although clearly visible from Blackpool on most days, the Lake District was always a considerable way away by land.

The next 'new' steamer acquired by the Furness Railway was the General Steam Navigation Co.'s *Philomel*. She had been built in 1889 for Thames services by the same company that built *Lady Evelyn*. She was larger than *Lady Margaret*, but was an unpopular steamer for the service and was soon nicknamed 'Full-o-smell' by regular travellers. She sailed with *Lady Evelyn* for the 1908 and 1909 seasons. *Philomel* finished the 1909 season on 18 September and it was then announced that she had 'not been a success and was not expected to sail again' and 'it was a pity she was ever put on the service'. She also required a new boiler estimated to cost £5,000. This cost was unacceptable and in January 1911 she was advertised for sale by auction. Reportedly purchased by T.W. Ward & Co for scrapping, this appears to have been premature as she was withdrawn from auction at £1,250. Little is known of *Philomel* after this until November 1913 when she was definitely sold to Ward's for £2,000 and scrapped.

After the disappointment of the *Philomel*, the Furness Railway purchased the Bristol Channel paddle steamer *Gwalia*. She was superior to the previous paddle steamers and had a speed of 19 knots. On a Class III certificate, she could accommodate 1,015 passengers. She changed her name from *Gwalia* to *Lady Moyra* on 26 May 1910.

The length of the *Lady Moyra* can be appreciated in this view as she approaches Fleetwood.

An evocative poster advertising the *Lady Moyra*. Such well-designed colour posters were sometimes supplemented by more novel means. In June 1910, Aslett purchased a model of *Gwalia* for £50 and had it mounted on wheels to be pushed around the streets of Blackpool to advertise his tours as well as using it for special events such as the Barrow hospital parades.

Lady Moyra was an immediate success and it was announced that a total of 128,000 passengers were carried on the Barrow to Fleetwood service in 1910. On 11 August 1911, *Lady Moyra* sailed to North Wales calling at Southport, Llandudno, Bangor and Menai Bridge. A total of 2,668 passengers were carried (not at the same time) and revenue was £198.

The colour posters produced by the Furness Railway were always of a high quality and more than amply promoted the beauty and romance of a cruise in Lakeland. The advertising was ahead of its time and must have helped the service achieve its popularity.

BARROW BOAT ARRIVING AT FLEETWOOD

Lady Margaret arriving at Fleetwood. The Saloon fare from Barrow to Blackpool was 4s 6d return. Weekly and monthly tickets were also available. A season ticket cost £2 in 1907. The season lasted from Whitsun until the end of September.

16563   *Gondola and Boat House, Coniston.*   J.V.

In 1859, the Furness Railway Co. built the *Gondola* for cruising on Coniston Water. The splendid vessel was the perfect marriage of a Venetian gondola and English steam yacht. The First Class Saloon was luxuriously decorated in walnut with sumptuous upholstery and gilded Corinthian columns at the windows. *Gondola* was withdrawn in 1936, but was magnificently rebuilt and returned to service in 1980 by the National Trust. Today, *Gondola* still operates as a graceful reminder of the Furness Railway and the days of the circular tour.

Like *Gondola*, *Lady of the Lake* was part of the Furness Railway 'Inner Circle Tour'. She had been launched in 1908 as a replacement for the ageing *Gondola*. But after public outcry, *Gondola* was never withdrawn. Both vessels carried on together until 1914. Captain Hamill became *Lady of the Lake*'s first master in 1908, after being master of *Gondola* for fifty years.

The steam yacht *Britannia* was the last vessel purchased by the Furness Railway in 1907 for service on Windermere. *Britannia* had originally been built as a private yacht by Seath's for Colonel Ridehalgh of Fell Foot. She was used as a charter vessel before the First World War and carried 122 passengers in considerable comfort often being serenaded by the 'Bateson's Orchestral Band'. Chartered pleasure steamers from the Fylde coast would sometimes arrange for passengers to be taken onwards from Barrow to Lakeside-on-Windermere to embark upon the *Britannia* for more intimate private cruises. She was laid up in 1915 and was scrapped in 1919.

Opposite: *Lady of the Lake* arriving at Lake Bank Pier, Coniston, ready to embark a good crowd ready for a cruise.

The most popular excursion offered by the Furness Railway was the 'Outer Circular Tour' as advertised on this poster from before the First World War. The next few images outline the route of this popular tour.

The starting point for the tour was Blackpool North Station. Trains left at 10.05 a.m. to take passengers to Fleetwood. Passengers then arrived here at Fleetwood Station ready to board the adjacent steamers. The funnel of one steamer can be seen on the left of this image.

The steamer was positioned close to the railway station. Passengers boarded steamers such as *Lady Evelyn*, leaving at 10.45 a.m. for the one-and-a-quarter-hour crossing of Morecambe Bay to Barrow.

From Ramsden Dock Station, a train left for the shores of Lake Windermere at Lakeside.

This photograph shows passengers that had just arrived at Lakeside Station by train. Here passengers usually enjoyed lunch. Diners were serenaded by 'Bateson's Orchestral Band' led by Thomas Bateson on cornet, his wife playing the violin and four other musicians. The ensemble had been started by Mr Bateson's father in 1859 and played on until the band ceased in 1915 due to the First World War. Bateson was furious with this decision, as none of his musicians was eligible for military service. After luncheon, most passengers boarded a steam yacht, such as the *Swift*, and from Lakeside, they sailed the full length of Windermere to Ambleside.

The next section of the tour was by horse-drawn coach to Coniston for a cruise, about 300 passengers being the largest number that could be conveyed. From Coniston the train was taken back to Barrow to connect with the steamer. This photograph shows passengers disembarking from the *Gondola* and the *Lady of the Lake* at Waterhead Pier, Coniston.

A postcard view. In the last pre-war season of 1913, the passenger figures had gone up to an astonishing 179,000 and in early 1914 a further rumour was heard that a large steamer to carry 1,500 was being contemplated. The service continued normally during the 1914 season, after which the *Lady Evelyn* and *Lady Moyra* were requisitioned for war service as minesweepers.

The Furness Railway guide for 1915 still advertised the Fleetwood to Barrow service but the advertisement was overprinted 'Deferred until further notice'. Both steamers survived the conflict and most assumed that the service would be resumed in 1919. However, a short announcement was made instead to say that sailings would not re-commence as the service had never been profitable and that conditions had changed. Coincidentally, Alfred Aslett, the architect of the steamer service, retired at this time. At first it was hoped that the Blackpool Passenger Steamboat Co. would consider taking over the Barrow to Fleetwood service, but this wasn't possible, except for a few trips from Barrow to Blackpool direct on Sundays and Bank Holidays commencing at Whitsun 1919. Thus, both *Lady Evelyn* and *Lady Moyra* were duly sold and the 'Lakeland Connection' ceased.

Do you recognise this paddle steamer? It is the *Lady Evelyn* in her later guise of *Brighton Belle*. After service with the Royal Navy, *Lady Evelyn* was sold to W.H. Tucker for further service on the Bristol Channel in 1919. She then moved to the South Coast and was renamed *Brighton Belle* in May 1923. She returned to the Bristol Channel in 1936 and in the following year her paddle box was renewed and the figure of the Madonna was removed from the crest (a reminder of her Furness Railway days). *Brighton Belle* served as a minesweeper from the outbreak of the Second World War, but was sunk whilst evacuating troops from Dunkirk at 1.00 p.m. on 28 May 1940. All of her crew were rescued by the *Medway Queen*.

Four
Years of Change

Atalanta was one of the last pleasure steamers to serve the Lancashire coast. The Second World War brought regular steamer services to an end, a quarter of a century before the demise of services elsewhere in the UK.

Robina was built for the Morecambe Central Pier Co. in 1914. After a short period, she was requisitioned by the Admiralty for use as a tender. *Robina* spent the 1919 season under charter to the Blackpool Passenger Steamboat Co. and, in the following year, spent the season on the Bristol Channel under charter to W.H. Tucker & Co., as well as spending the winter sailing between Cardiff and Bristol. *Robina* returned to the Blackpool station for the 1923 season under charter to the Blackpool Steam Shipping Co. and then in 1924 to her rival of the previous season, H. Douglas Bickerstaffe.

A postcard view of *Robina* approaching Blackpool Central Pier. After her two years at Blackpool, *Robina* was sold on 8 January 1925 to Belfast owners and then spent a long life in various guises around the coast of the UK.

Tynwald III at Blackpool North Pier loading a good crowd for a cruise. The Isle of Man Steam Packet Co.'s *Tynwald III* received permission to cruise from the jetty during the 1929 season. Unfortunately, the *Tynwald III* was unsuitable for Blackpool trade and terminated the season on 18 September. *Tynwald III* was at this time quite elderly having originally been built in 1891. She was the first steamer built for the Isle of Man Steam Packet Co. with a triple-expansion engine and electric lighting. (Photo courtesy of Leisure Parcs Ltd)

Snowdon approaching Blackpool North Pier. The Middle Walk collonades and Warley Road are off the port paddle box with Norbreck and Cleveleys off the bow. Note the deckhands poised to throw the lines in order to secure the *Snowdon* to the jetty.

Between the withdrawal of *Bickerstaffe* in 1928 and the commencement in service of *Minden* in 1933, Blackpool was without a regular pleasure steamer service for the first time in seventy years. There were a few cruises by the *Tynwald III* in 1929. Also during July 1930, HM battlecruiser *Tiger* paid a courtesy visit to Blackpool and the pier company arranged with the North Wales Steamship Co. to ply from the jetty to view the battlecruiser during her stay. The only other vessel to serve the North Pier was the *Snowdon*. She offered cruises from the pier in September 1930 to view the illuminations. *Snowdon* was operated by the Liverpool & North Wales Co. and was an attractive paddle steamer that could carry 462 passengers. This image shows the large awning on the promenade deck that could be unfolded when weather was poor.

The early 1930s saw few pleasure cruises along the Lancashire coast. However, in 1933 Blackpool Pleasure Steamers Ltd changed this when they acquired the Mersey ferry *Old Bidston* for further service along the Lancashire coast from Blackpool. *Old Bidston* is seen here against Liverpool's famous waterfront.

Old Bidston was renamed *Minden* and undertook a range of short cruises from Blackpool North Pier to such familiar destinations as Morecambe Bay. She made her first sailing from North Pier in July 1933. Here, a smart-looking *Minden* is crowded with passengers who are ready to disembark.

Minden approaching North Pier. In the distance, the Middle Walk collonades and Warley Road can be seen at the bow with the Queens Promenade and the dome of the Savoy Hotel behind *Minden*'s funnel. The loading of local suppliers' stores often caused problems. Errand boys often found themselves transporting the stores from the shop along the pier and then down several flights of steps. Often cruises were cancelled and the stores had to then be carried back along the arduous route.

The beach at Morecambe in the 1930s with the old stone jetty beyond.

JETTY BOATING POOL, MORECAMBE.

Minden departing from Morecambe's stone jetty for Blackpool's North Pier in the mid-1930s.
This jetty was later used by the *Balmoral*, thus reviving similar cruises from the early 1930s.

S.S. "QUEEN OF THE BAY."

In 1935 *Queen of the Bay* was acquired for Blackpool service. She sailed from South Africa on an epic ninety-eight-day voyage to Liverpool where she arrived in December 1935. She made her first trip from North Pier on 26 July 1936. The day before, an inaugural civic cruise had been organised. Unfortunately, *Queen of the Bay* didn't arrive in time and the civic party had to be entertained on *Minden* before travelling home, without sampling the new vessel!

Opposite: Aerial view showing the Tower and North Pier jetty in the 1940s. The Sun Lounge and Theatre were rebuilt at the pier head in the 1930s and remain to this day. The jetty was being used less frequently from the 1920s, but survived until the 1990s.

Jubilee Queen (left) and *Minden* (right) at Blackpool North Pier jetty during the summer

of 1936. (Photo courtesy of Leisure Parcs Ltd)

Queen of the Bay was 220ft long, travelled at 18 knots and carried about 750 passengers. Her dining saloon could seat 120 and her lounge 90. For her first Blackpool season, 1936, she had a white hull and yellow funnel. The following year her hull was painted black with a black topping to her funnel. On 23 October 1937, it was reported that she had been sold and was already bound for a French port. She was clearly not suited to Lancashire coast trade on account of her build and heavy running costs.

A 1936 postal cover showing an image of the *Jubilee Queen* as well as the signature of Captain Kearney.

Opposite: Jubilee Queen was named in honour of the Silver Jubilee of King George V in 1935. Originally built in 1897 as *Duchess of Kent*, she was sold and renamed as *Clacton Queen* in 1933. She was acquired by the Mersey & Blackpool Steamship Co. and cruised from Liverpool and New Brighton to Blackpool and Fleetwood at Easter 1936 and then for a further short period at the end of May.

Jubilee Queen was transferred to the Jubilee Shipping Co. and undertook several trips from Liverpool to Blackpool during July. She was then sold to Mr S. Kelley and sailed from Barrow to Fleetwood, as well as a few cruises to Blackpool until 13 September. *Jubilee Queen* was scrapped at Preston in May 1937.

Atalanta was originally built for the Glasgow & South Western Railway Co. in 1906 for service on the Firth of Clyde. She continued to cruise these waters until 1936 when she was deemed to be in poor condition. Some £2,136 was required for annual maintenance.

Despite her poor condition, *Atalanta* was sold in the spring of 1937 to the Blackpool Steam Navigation Co. for the sum of £3,000 as a 'going proposition'. Despite her obvious defects and condition, *Atalanta* spent the next two summers cruising from Blackpool North Pier to such favourite destinations as Llandudno and Fleetwood, as well as reviving the classic cruise to Barrow where she linked in with Lake District tours of the London, Midland & Scottish Railway. She also sailed to Morecambe, having re-started cruises from the town's pier on 23 May 1937, some twenty-three years after the last departure.

With the withdrawal of *Minden* and *Queen of the Bay* in October 1937, *Atalanta* was left alone to carry on cruising from North Pier until the outbreak of the Second World War. *Atalanta* was requisitioned on 8 June 1940 for net-laying and boom inspection duties. She never returned to Blackpool after the war and was taken to Methil and from there to the inevitable scrapyard of Van Heygen Freres in Ghent. *Atalanta* was Blackpool's last large pleasure steamer.

Pendennis was acquired by the Blackpool Steam Navigation Co. (1947) Ltd in 1947. *Pendennis* was a former Fairmile launch built for the Admiralty in 1940. Here she is seen approaching the North Pier jetty during her short career at Blackpool. She was the last Blackpool pleasure boat. After her withdrawal, it would be another forty-five years before *Balmoral* offered cruises from North Pier again. (Photo courtesy of Leisure Parcs Ltd)

Five

The Story Continues

Balmoral at Blackpool North Pier on 10 May 1994 prior to departure on a cruise to Barrow. Pleasure-steamer sailings were revived on the Lancashire coast by the motor vessel *Balmoral* and the paddle steamer *Waverley*. (Picture courtesy of *The Gazette*, Blackpool)

The Clyde-based *Waverley* was approached in late 1976 to take part in the centenary celebrations of Llandudno Pier in May 1977. The shortness of the Clyde season meant that this was an ideal opportunity to look at new markets away from her traditional waters. Plans were being drawn up when Aberconwy Council withdrew their financial backing. By this stage enough enthusiasm had been shown and *Waverley*'s operating company decided to push on with plans to take her to the Irish Sea as planned. *Waverley* is shown here open to the public at Liverpool on Saturday 30 April 1977.

Perhaps one of the most dramatic scenes of that momentous week was when *Waverley* sailed to Fleetwood from Liverpool for a Morecambe Bay cruise on Sunday 8 May 1977. The whole town of Fleetwood seemed to turn out to welcome a paddle steamer back to the port. For a few spectators, it must have bought back nostalgic memories of cruises from the town by such steamers as *Lady Evelyn*, *Lady Margaret* and *Greyhound* in the halcyon days before the First World War.

Opposite: Waverley duly left Campbeltown on Thursday 28 April 1977 and arrived at the Princes Landing Stage, Liverpool, at 4.30 p.m. the following day. This photograph shows *Waverley* at Liverpool with the Isle of Man Steam Packet Co.'s *Ben my Chree* at her stern and the famous Mersey ferry *Royal Iris* sailing past.

111

The official celebrations and *Waverley*'s raison d'être for visiting the Irish Sea was the centenary of Llandudno's magnificent pier. *Waverley* made that first historic call at 2.00 p.m. on 1 May 1977 with a full complement of passengers from Liverpool. She is seen here returning to Llandudno at the end of the cruise. More successful cruises were offered during the week for schools, pensioners and the public and several charters were undertaken.

As *Waverley* departed from Fleetwood, the sheer success of the week was a clear indication that *Waverley* should spend a significant part of her sailing year away from the Clyde in order to maximise her revenue. *Waverley* returned to Fleetwood in April 1980, undertaking cruises in Morecambe Bay. On Sunday 20 April 1980, 842 passengers boarded for an afternoon cruise from Liverpool to Fleetwood for a Morecambe Bay cruise.

Opposite: Waverley berthing at Fleetwood on 8 May 1977. One man in the crowd muttered to a local reporter, 'If I had £5 for everyone here, I would be a rich man.' What better confirmation for the wisdom and gamble taken by *Waverley*'s operating company than to see such crowds at Fleetwood on this day!

Waverley at Heysham on 11 April 1979. *Waverley* stopped at Heyham for refuelling overnight on Monday 10/Tuesday 11 April. She had departed from Glasgow on Sunday and finally arrived on Friday 14 April after a stormy passage. Note the 'whiteness' of her hull as storm covers are in place over her saloon windows on the main deck.

St Anne's Pier suffered from catastrophic fires in the 1970s and 1980s that destroyed its famous and exotic pavilions. As a result of this, the seaward end was demolished, leaving the steamer jetty isolated as a reminder of past glories.

Opposite: Waverley berthed at Heysham in April 1979. *Waverley* was due to make an inaugural call at North Pier, Blackpool, in May 1992, but this had to be cancelled. Hopefully, Waverley will one day make another call at Fleetwood as a reminder of past Lancashire paddle steamers.

St Anne's steamer jetty, photographed in December 2002. The shifting sands were the main reason for the cessation of services from St Anne's. The image on page 56 shows that the jetty once had several landing levels. These have long disappeared beneath the shifting sands.

Opposite: Passengers disembarking from *Balmoral* as the sun sets against Blackpool North Pier on 9 May 1994. Balmoral had just returned from a cruise to Llandudno and the Menai Bridge.

Although the last pleasure steamer called at the pier around eighty years ago, the original fittings remain. Posts, bollards and gratings give a feeling of what it must have been like in the heyday of the Lancashire pleasure steamers. St Anne's Pier jetty is perhaps the only (if derelict) reminder of those days, now that most of the other jetties have been destroyed.

Balmoral's brochure for Lancashire coast cruises in 1992.

118

Balmoral arriving at North Pier, Blackpool on 20 September 1992 from Llandudno. She embarked her passengers at 2.00 p.m. for a three-hour cruise to Morecambe Bay to view the mountains of the Lake District. This was a particularly successful day, with 761 passengers sailing during the day. (Picture courtesy of *The Gazette*, Blackpool)

Balmoral leaving North Pier on 20 September 1992. After such a lengthy absence, many holidaymakers must have stood in amazement as *Balmoral* approached the jetty. *Balmoral* had originally been built for service between Southampton and Cowes in 1949. In a varied career, she had spent some time working in North Wales, as well as acting as a tender in June 1975, as liners were too large to enter a port such as Fleetwood. *Balmoral* was an ideal tender to take passengers ashore to their excursions to Blackpool and the Lake District. After withdrawal from service in 1980, *Balmoral* faced an uncertain future, including a brief spell as a floating restaurant and disco before finally being purchased and restored as a consort to *Waverley* in 1986. (Picture courtesy of *The Gazette*, Blackpool)

All Aboard the Balmoral
First Ever Cruises from Barrow!

Welcome aboard the beautiful motor pleasure cruiser BALMORAL, the UK's Most Widely Travelled Excursion Ship, on her first ever cruises from Barrow-in-Furness this May! With a special 5 day programme, you can sail with us from Whitehaven or Barrow to the magical Isle of Man – the "Treasured Isle" – or soak up the atmosphere on an Evening Showboat Cruise! Owned by a charity, this unique & historic ship was built in 1949 – British Registered for 680 passengers with self service restaurant, lounge bars, souvenir shop & sun decks! Don't Miss a Great Trip for all the Family!!!

from BARROW IN FURNESS – Belfast Berth

FIRST EVER SAILINGS - MORECAMBE BAY & FYLDE COAST

FRIDAY MAY 11 LEAVE 2pm back 5.30pm
Enjoy a unique afternoon cruise aboard Balmoral viewing the Golden Sands of Morecambe Bay, Fylde Coastline & the popular seaside resort of Blackpool turning off the world famous Blackpool Tower £11.95. Senior Citizens £9.95.

EVENING SHOWBOAT CRUISE - LANCASHIRE COAST & MORECAMBE BAY

FRIDAY MAY 11 LEAVE 7pm back 10.30pm
Don't Miss this Great Night Out!! Soak up the atmosphere as the Jazzband entertains you on this special evening showboat cruise of the Lancashire Coast & Morecambe Bay £13.95. Make it a party – groups of 10 adults or more £12.55 each!!

DAY TRIP TO THE ISLE OF MAN

SATURDAY MAY 12 LEAVE 11am back 10.30pm
Don't miss Balmoral's first Grand Day Cruise from Barrow across the Irish Sea to visit the magical Isle of Man - spend a glorious afternoon in Douglas, the Island's Capital, with its sandy beaches, trams & steam railway £23.95. SC £21.95.

from WHITEHAVEN North Pier

"Kids Free Today" - AFTERNOON CRUISE, ST. BEES HEAD

SUNDAY MAY 13 LEAVE 2pm back 5pm
Grand Afternoon trip, cruising down the Cumbrian Coast – Cliffs & Headlands to view famous St. Bees Head £12.95. Senior Citizens £10.95. *One child travels free with every adult ticket purchased.*

DAY TRIP TO THE ISLE OF MAN – VINTAGE STEAM RAILWAY
Senior Citizens - "Bring a Friend FREE" to Douglas on 18 May

FRIDAY MAY 18 & SATURDAY MAY 19 LEAVE 10am back 9pm
Day trip to visit Douglas – Isle of Man £22.95. Or enjoy the Grand Full Day Cruise – see the beautiful Island Coast – the Calf of Man – spectacular Calf Sound - £27.95 Sen Cits £23.95. Or cruise to Douglas to join the Vintage Steam Railway – opened in 1874 – for a thrilling Steam train trip through the Island countryside to charming resort of Port St. Mary where you re-join Balmoral to cruise home. Inclusive fare £29.95 Sen Cits £25.95. *On May 18 Senior Citizens are invited to "Bring a Friend Free" to Douglas – 1 free ticket for each ticket purchased!!*

ISLE OF MAN MINI BREAK

Enjoy a cruise of discovery for an Isle of Man mini holiday, leaving Friday morning 10am and returning Saturday evening 9pm – Period return cruise ticket only £42.95. Please note that no accommodation is included in this price.

BE SURE OF YOUR TICKETS – BOOK NOW
By Visa – Mastercard – Switch - Telephone 0141-243-2224

Or post your cheque to Waverley Excursions Ltd, Waverley Terminal, Anderston Quay, Glasgow. Tickets will be posted to you, or, if time is short, will be available to collect when you board your cruise. Or Book through your local Tourist Information Centres at: Barrow, Whitehaven, Workington, Carlisle, Maryport or Buy Your Tickets On Board Balmoral When You Sail

Waverley Excursions Limited, Waverley Terminal, Anderston Quay, Glasgow – in association with the Paddle Steamer Preservation Society - A Charity. All bookings are taken, tickets issued & all passengers & others carried subject to the terms & conditions of Waverley Excursions Ltd. Copies available on request from the Company's offices or on demand from the Purser at the gangway before going on board. All sailings are subject to weather, visibility & circumstances permitting. Catering offered subject to availability. An alternative may be provided for any sailings, routes & destinations may be altered, if weather conditions make this necessary. No passenger under the influence of alcohol will be allowed to board the ship & no alcohol may be brought on board. No refunds can be made for tickets purchased for sailings that take place, but unused tickets can be used, up to the purchase value, towards any alternative sailing. Passengers are entitled to a full refund for the value of any tickets booked for a sailing which is cancelled or can retain the ticket for use on any other public sailing at no extra charge.

Waverley & Balmoral are owned by a Charity

Balmoral's brochure detailing her first cruises from Barrow-in-Furness along with cruises from Whitehaven.

Balmoral departing on a Morecambe Bay cruise from Blackpool, reviving a tradition set by such notable names as *Greyhound* and *Queen of the North*. Today, *Balmoral* is Britain's widest travelled excursion ship and tirelessly travels around the whole of the UK each summer to support *Waverley* and to keep alive the tradition of coastal excursions. Sadly, the North Pier jetty was severely damaged by a storm in December 1997 and has since been demolished. *Balmoral* still carries out regular cruises from traditional pleasure steamer points such as Barrow, Llandudno, Douglas and Liverpool.

Morecambe's Midland Railway Pier viewed from the bridge deck of *Balmoral* as the vessel makes her approach at 3.00 p.m. on 6 June 1993. *Balmoral* had left Menai Bridge at 8.30 a.m. and made calls at Llandudno and Blackpool. She had carried over 600 passengers on this occasion. Unfortunately, recent sea defence works in the vicinity of the pier has made further calls difficult.

A view from *Balmoral* as she arrives back at Blackpool North Pier from a cruise to Llandudno in 1992. Passengers are about to embark for the cruise back to Morecambe.

Captain Steve Michel on the bridge of *Balmoral* during the first visit to Blackpool in 1992. Captain Michel was *Balmoral*'s regular master from her return to service in 1986 until the early 1990s.

A rare aerial view of *Balmoral* tied up on Blackpool's North Pier. The jetty in the 1990s was smaller than the one ninety years earlier. One obstacle to embarkation in the 1990s was the landing platform for the helicopter that offered sightseeing flights around the resort and Tower from the pier jetty. Passengers can be seen negotiating this platform as they board *Balmoral*. The North Pier has retained its wide expanse of decking for promenading, but a small train now operates to take people to the pier head.

Opposite: Balmoral's passengers watch with interest as she is secured to Blackpool North Pier in 1992.

Balmoral alongside at North Pier, Blackpool. On several occasions, *Balmoral* tied up at a right angle to the jetty instead of alongside. The lack of bollards and other facilities made docking a challenge. Gratings had also been removed from the deck of the jetty and a walkway was constructed down the centre.

Modes of transport from different ages converge at Fleetwood in 1980 as *Waverley* departs for a cruise.

Lady of Mann arriving at Fleetwood in the 1990s. Fleetwood's link with the Isle of Man began at the earliest stages of the port's development. Most of the Isle of Man Steam Packet Co.'s ships served on the Fleetwood to Douglas route at some time. In the 1980s and 1990s, ships such as the *Lady of Mann* and *Mona's Queen* offered 'Fun Boat' excursions to the island with inclusive entertainment. Now, the service is almost non-existent with just one or two cruises being offered from Fleetwood each year.

Several attempts to introduce a hovercraft service have been made over the years. This photograph shows a short-lived service at St Anne's in July 1991. This service ran to Southport as well as to the neighbouring South Pier at Blackpool.

The bell of the *Bickerstaffe* has survived and is now on display at Blackpool Central Library along with a painting of the *Bickerstaffe* in her heyday. Blackpool North Pier also houses a heritage centre at the pier head showing the past glories of the pier and the pleasure steamers that once used it.

Minden approaches Blackpool North Pier against a glorious Irish Sea sunset in 1935. By this time, the golden era of pleasure steamers on the Lancashire coast was disappearing like the sun at the end of this summer day. The coastline had witnessed a frenzied explosion of pleasure steamers of all sizes over a relatively short space of time that coincided itself with the Victorian boom in the resorts themselves. These steamers witnessed some of the most spectacular cruises available in the UK and gave those innocent 'Wakes Week' trippers an adventure that they would always remember. By the time that this photograph was taken, this era was almost at an end. But, thankfully, the story doesn't end with this picture. For it is still possible on a few occasions each year to sample these innocent pleasures aboard the *Balmoral* or *Waverley* as the classic cruises of the *Greyhound, Belle* and *Lady Evelyn* are recreated! (Photo courtesy of Leisure Parcs Ltd)